TREATS

just great recipes

GENERAL INFORMATION

The level of difficulty of the recipes in this book
is expressed as a number from 1 (simple) to 3 (difficult).

chocolate

McRae Books

MAKES about 40 pieces

PREPARATION 5 min + 2 h to set

COOKING 20 min

DIFFICULTY level 1

Black and White
chocolates

Line an 8 x 10-inch (20 x 23-cm) baking pan with waxed paper. • Melt the white chocolate in a double boiler over barely simmering water. Add the butter and mix until smooth and glossy. Remove from the heat. • Melt the bittersweet chocolate in a double boiler over barely simmering water. • Place alternate spoonfuls of the white chocolate and bittersweet chocolate in the prepared pan. Swirl the two together with a knife to create a marbled effect. • Let the chocolate cool at room temperature until set, about 2 hours. • Cut into small squares and serve.

12 oz (350 g) white chocolate
$^1/_2$ cup (125 g) butter
14 oz (400 g) bittersweet (dark) chocolate

MAKES about 40 pieces

PREPARATION 20 min + 3 h 20 min to cool

COOKING 20 min

DIFFICULTY level 2

Chocolate
caramel fudge

Butter an 8-inch (20-cm) square baking pan. • Place the sugar, brown sugar, chocolate, corn syrup, cream, and milk in a large, heavy-based saucepan over low heat. Stir until the sugar has melted, taking care not to let the mixture boil. When the sugar has completely melted, bring to a boil and simmer over low heat for 10 minutes. • Remove from the heat and add the butter. Do not stir the mixture at this stage. Let cool for 20 minutes. • Stir with a wooden spoon until very thick, about 10 minutes. • Pour into the prepared pan. Cover with a piece of baking parchment and let cool until set, about 3 hours. • Turn out onto a cutting board. Cut into small squares.

1½ cups (300 g) sugar
½ cup (100 g) firmly packed brown sugar
3 oz (90 g) bittersweet (dark) chocolate, chopped
2 tablespoons corn (golden) syrup
½ cup (125 ml) heavy (double) cream
¼ cup (60 ml) milk
¼ cup (60 g) butter

MAKES 16 miniature cupcakes

PREPARATION 20 min + 15 min to chill

COOKING 10 min

DIFFICULTY level 2

Mini Chocolate
cupcakes with cream and fruit

Set out 16 miniature paper cupcake cases. • Melt the chocolate in a double boiler over barely simmering water. • Use a pastry brush to paint the paper cases with a thick layer of chocolate. • Chill in the refrigerator until the chocolate has set, about 15 minutes. • Carefully peel the paper cases away from the chocolate and discard them. • Place the chocolate cases on a serving dish. • Beat the mascarpone and liqueur in a bowl. • Use a teaspoon to fill the chocolate cases with the cream. • Decorate each one with a raspberry and a blueberry. • Chill until ready to serve.

5 oz (150 g) semisweet (dark) chocolate, broken into pieces
$2/3$ cup (150 g) mascarpone cheese
1 tablespoon orange liqueur
16 fresh raspberries
16 fresh blueberries

Chocolate Rice
crispies with nuts

Set out 16–20 miniature paper cupcake cases. • Melt the chocolate and butter in a double boiler over barely simmering water. • Remove from the heat and add the almonds and hazelnuts. • Stir in the puffed rice and mix well. • Spoon the mixture into the paper cupcake cases. • Chill in the refrigerator for 1 hour before serving.

8 oz (250 g) semisweet (dark) chocolate, broken into pieces

2/3 cup (150 g) butter

1/2 cup (50 g) chopped almonds

1/2 cup (50 g) chopped hazelnuts

1 3/4 cups (100 g) puffed rice

Chocolate

truffles

Beat the butter and confectioners' sugar in a medium bowl until pale and creamy • Beat in the egg yolks one at a time. • Bring the cream to the boil. Remove from the heat and add the vanilla. • Pour the boiling cream into the butter mixture. Add the chocolate and stir until smooth and well mixed. • Let cool for at least 2 hours. • Shape into balls the size of small walnuts. • Roll one-third of the truffles in the cocoa, one-third in the coconut, and one-third in the nuts. • Chill in the refrigerator until ready to serve.

$1/4$ cup (60 g) butter, softened

$1/3$ cup (50 g) confectioners' (icing) sugar

2 large egg yolks

$1/3$ cup (50 g) heavy (double) cream

1 teaspoon vanilla extract (essence)

12 oz (350 g) bittersweet (dark) chocolate, grated

3 tablespoons unsweetened cocoa powder

3 tablespoons shredded (dessicated) coconut

3 tablespoons chopped hazelnuts

MAKES 16–20

PREPARATION 25 min + 4 h to chill

COOKING 10 min

DIFFICULTY level 1

White Chocolate
cheesecake slice with raspberries

Line an 8-inch (20-cm) square baking pan with waxed paper. • Mix the cookies, butter, and cinnamon in a large bowl. Press the mixture into the prepared baking pan, leveling it with the back of a spoon. Chill in the refrigerator while you prepare the filling. • Melt the chocolate in a double boiler over barely simmering water. • Dissolve the gelatin in the boiling water. • Beat the cream cheese and sugar in a large bowl until smooth. • Stir in the cream and vanilla. Mix well. • Add the gelatin and chocolate and mix well. • Pour the filling over the prepared base. Sprinkle with the raspberries. • Chill in the refrigerator for 4 hours. • Cut into squares and serve.

5 oz (150 g) ladyfinger cookies, crumbled

1/3 cup (90 g) butter, melted

1 teaspoon ground cinnamon

5 oz (150 g) white chocolate, chopped

1 tablespoon gelatin powder

3 tablespoons boiling water

6 oz (180 g) cream cheese

1/2 cup (100 g) sugar

1 cup (250 ml) heavy (double) cream

1/2 teaspoon vanilla extract (essence)

12 oz (350 g) fresh raspberries

MAKES 30–36

PREPARATION 30 min + 6 h to chill

COOKING 10 min

DIFFICULTY level 1

White Chocolate
nut and raspberry squares

Line a 9-inch (23-cm) square baking pan with aluminum foil. Brush the foil with almond oil. • Melt the chocolate with the condensed milk, butter, and maple syrup in a double boiler over barely simmering water. • Remove from the heat and let cool for 20 minutes, stirring from time to time. • Pour the mixture into the prepared pan. • Sprinkle with the raspberries pressing them into the chocolate with your fingertips. Sprinkle with flaked almonds. • Cover and chill in the refrigerator for 6 hours. • Turn out onto a cutting board. Remove the foil. • Cut into small squares using a sharp knife dipped in boiling water.

1 lb (500 g) white chocolate, chopped
1⅓ cups (350 ml) condensed milk
¼ cup (60 g) butter
1 tablespoon maple syrup
3 oz (90 g) fresh raspberries
2 tablespoons flaked almonds, toasted

MAKES 12 muffins

PREPARATION 15 min

COOKING 30 min

DIFFICULTY level 2

Chocolate
marbled muffins

Preheat the oven to 350°F (180°C/gas 4). • Butter a 12-cup muffin. • Melt the both chocolates in a double boiler over barely simmering water. • Beat the eggs, yogurt, sugar, vanilla, and butter in a large bowl until smooth and creamy. • Add the flour, baking powder, and salt, stirring until well mixed. • Place alternate spoonfuls of the batter and chocolate mixture in the muffin cups. Use the blade of a knife to swirl the batter in each muffin case to create a marbled effect. • Bake until well risen and springy to the touch, about 20 minutes. • Let cool slightly. Turn out onto a rack and let cool completely.

3 oz (90 g) semisweet (dark) chocolate, chopped

4 oz (125 g) hazelnut chocolate, chopped

2 large eggs

Generous ³/₄ cup (200 g) plain yogurt

¹/₂ cup (100 g) sugar

¹/₂ teaspoon vanilla extract (essence)

¹/₃ cup (90 g) butter, melted

1²/₃ cups (250 g) all-purpose (plain) flour

2 teaspoons baking powder

¹/₄ teaspoon salt

Chocolate
almond cupcakes

Preheat the oven to 350°F (180°C/gas 4). • Set out 8–10 paper cupcake cases. • Beat the egg yolks and sugar in a large bowl until pale and creamy. • Beat in the flour, baking powder, and cocoa. • Beat the egg whites in a large bowl until stiff. Fold into the chocolate mixture. • Fold in the almonds. • Spoon the batter into the cupcake cases. • Bake until well risen and springy to the touch, 15–20 minutes. • Place on a cooling rack. Let cool completely. • Melt the preserves and water in a small saucepan over low heat. Brush each cupcake with this mixture. • Frosting: Place the confectioners' sugar, cocoa, and butter in a bowl. Stir in enough boiling water to make a spreadable frosting. • Spread the cupcakes with the frosting and let set.

3 large eggs, separated
1/2 cup (100 g) sugar
2/3 cup (100 g) all-purpose (plain) flour
1/3 cup (50 g) unsweetened cocoa powder
1 teaspoon baking powder
1/2 cup (50 g) finely chopped almonds
1/2 cup (125 g) apricot preserves (jam)
2 tablespoons water

Frosting
1 1/2 cups (225 g) confectioners' (icing) sugar
4 tablespoons unsweetened cocoa powder
2 tablespoons butter, softened
2–4 tablespoons boiling water

Chocolate
nut muffins

Preheat the oven to 350°F (180°C/gas 4). • Butter a 12-cup muffin pan. • Sift the flour and baking powder into a bowl. Add the almonds and hazelnuts. • Melt two-thirds of the chocolate in a double boiler over barely simmering water. • Beat the chocolate, eggs, milk, sugar, and oil in a large bowl. • Stir in the mixed dry ingredients, mixing well. • Spoon the batter into the prepared pan. • Bake until well risen and springy to the touch, 15–20 minutes. • Let cool slightly before turning out onto a wire rack. Let cool completely. • Melt the remaining chocolate in a double boiler over barely simmering water. • Spread each muffin with some of the chocolate and let set.

1 1/3 cups (200 g) all-purpose (plain) flour

2 teaspoons baking powder

1/2 cup (50 g) finely chopped almonds

1 1/2 cups (150 g) coarsely chopped hazelnuts

12 oz (350 g) semisweet (dark) chocolate, broken into pieces

2 large eggs

Scant 1 1/4 cups (300 ml) milk

3/4 cup (150 g) sugar

1/3 cup (90 ml) sunflower oil

MAKES 10–12

PREPARATION 25 min + 1 h to chill

COOKING 20 min

DIFFICULTY level 2

Chocolate
hazelnut kisses

Beat the butter, vanilla, sugar, and egg in a large bowl until pale and creamy. • Stir in the flour, hazelnuts, and cocoa to obtain a firm dough. • Shape into a ball and wrap in plastic wrap (cling film). Chill in the refrigerator for 1 hour • Preheat the oven to 350°F (180°C/gas 4). • Oil 2 baking sheets. • Roll out the dough to ⅛ inch (3 mm) thick. Cut into 2-inch (5-cm) disks using a cookie cutter. • Arrange on the prepared baking sheets. • Bake, one sheet at a time, until lightly browned, about 10 minutes. • Remove from the oven and let cool for 5 minutes. Transfer to a cooling rack and let cool completely. • Chocolate Hazelnut Filling: Melt the chocolate in a double boiler over barely simmering water. • Beat the chocolate, butter, and hazelnut spread in a bowl until smooth. • Chill in the refrigerator for 20 minutes. • Spread half the cooled cookies with the filling. Cover with the remaining cookies. • Dust with cocoa before serving.

⅓ cup (90 g) butter, softened
1 teaspoon vanilla extract (essence)
⅓ cup (70 g) sugar
1 large egg
¾ cup (125 g) all-purpose (plain) flour
½ cup (50 g) ground hazelnuts
¼ cup (30 g) unsweetened cocoa powder + extra, to dust

Chocolate Hazelnut Filling
4 oz (125 g) semisweet (dark) chocolate, broken into pieces
Scant ¼ cup (50 g) butter
4 oz (125 g) chocolate hazelnut spread

Chocolate
walnut cupcakes

Preheat the oven to 350°F (180°C/gas 4). • Set out 12 paper cupcake cases. • Melt the chocolate and butter in a double boiler over barely simmering water. • Add the sugar and egg yolks. Beat until smooth and glossy. Remove from the heat and let cool. • Beat the egg whites in a large bowl until stiff. • Fold the egg whites, flour, and baking powder into the chocolate mixture. • Divide the mixture among the cupcake cases. • Top each one with walnuts • Bake until well risen and springy to the touch, 15–20 minutes. • Serve warm.

8 oz (250 g) semisweet (dark) chocolate, broken into pieces
$1/3$ cup (90 g) butter
$1/2$ cup (100 g) sugar
3 large eggs, separated
$1/2$ cup (75 g) all-purpose (plain) flour
$1/2$ teaspoon baking powder
$1/2$ cup (60 g) walnuts, coarsely chopped

MAKES 12

PREPARATION 15 min

COOKING 25 min

DIFFICULTY level 2

Chocolate
mango muffins

Preheat the oven to 350°F (180°C/gas 4). • Butter a 12-cup muffin pan. • Sift the flour, cocoa, and baking powder into a bowl. • Add the mango and chocolate chips and mix well. • Beat the eggs, yogurt, sugar, and oil in a bowl until smooth. • Add the flour mixture and stir until all the ingredients are well incorporated. • Spoon half the batter into the muffin cups. Add some hazelnut spread to each muffin and cover with the remaining batter. • Bake until well risen and springy to the touch, 15–20 minutes. • Let cool slightly before turning out onto a wire rack. Serve warm or at room temperature.

1²/₃ cups (250 g) all-purpose (plain) flour
¹/₃ cup (50 g) unsweetened cocoa powder
2 teaspoons baking powder
8 oz (250 g) chopped fresh mango
2 oz (60 g) semisweet (dark) chocolate chips
2 large eggs
1 cup (250 g) plain yogurt
¹/₂ cup (100 g) sugar
¹/₃ cup (90 ml) sunflower oil
4 oz (125 g) chocolate hazelnut spread

MAKES 30–35

PREPARATION 30 min + 30 min to set

COOKING 30 min

DIFFICULTY level 2

White Chocolate

florentines

Preheat the oven to 325°F (170°C/gas 3). • Spread the hazelnuts on a large baking sheet. Toast until pale gold, 7–10 minutes. • Transfer to a food processor with 1/4 cup (50 g) of sugar and process until very finely chopped. • Increase the oven temperature to 375°F (190°C/gas 5). • Set out three baking sheets. • Melt the butter with the honey, cream, and remaining sugar in a small saucepan over low heat until the sugar has dissolved completely. • Bring to a boil and boil for 2 minutes. • Remove from the heat and stir in the nut mixture and salt. • Drop teaspoons of the mixture 3 inches (8 cm) apart on the cookie sheets. • Bake, one sheet at a time, until golden brown, 8–10 minutes. • Cool on the sheets for 5 minutes, then transfer to cooling racks and let cool completely. • Melt the white chocolate in a double boiler over barely simmering water. • Spread one side of each cookie with white chocolate. • Melt the semisweet chocolate in a double boiler over barely simmering water. • Drizzle over the white chocolate. • Let stand until set, about 30 minutes.

1 lb (500 g) hazelnuts
1 cup (200 g) sugar
1 cup (250 g) butter, softened
1/2 cup (125 g) honey
1/2 cup (125 ml) heavy (double) cream
1/8 teaspoon salt
6 oz (180 g) white chocolate, coarsely chopped
4 oz (125 g) semisweet (dark) chocolate, coarsely chopped

Simple Brownies

Preheat the oven to 350°F (180°C/gas 4). • Butter a 9-inch (23-cm) square baking pan. • Beat the eggs and sugar in a large bowl until pale and creamy. • Add the butter gradually, beating constantly. Add the vanilla. • Fold in the flour, cocoa, and salt. • Spoon the batter into the prepared pan. Sprinkle with the white chocolate. • Bake until almost firm to the touch, about 30 minutes. • Let cool in the pan on a rack. • Cut into squares.

4 large eggs
2¼ cups (450 g) sugar
Generous ¾ cup (200 g) butter, melted
1 teaspoon vanilla extract (essence)
1 cup (150 g) all-purpose (plain) flour
⅔ cup (100 g) unsweetened cocoa
¼ teaspoon salt
2 oz (60 g) white chocolate, grated

MAKES about 20

PREPARATION 20 min

COOKING 40 min

DIFFICULTY level 1

Rich Brownies
with pecans

Preheat the oven to 350°F (180°C/gas 4). • Butter an 8-inch (20-cm) square baking pan. • Sift the flour and salt into a medium bowl. • Melt the semisweet chocolate and butter in a double boiler over barely simmering water. • Transfer to a medium bowl and let cool for 5 minutes. • Mix in the white and milk chocolate chips and the pecans. • Add the eggs one at a time, beating until just blended. • Mix in the dry ingredients. • Spoon the batter into the prepared pan. • Bake until dry on top and almost firm to the touch. • Let cool in the pan on a rack. • Cut into squares.

1½ cups (225 g) all-purpose (plain) flour
⅛ tsp salt
8 oz (250 g) semisweet (dark) chocolate, coarsely chopped
½ cup (125 g) butter, cut up
1 cup (180 g) white chocolate chips
1 cup (180 g) milk chocolate chips
1 cup (100 g) coarsely chopped pecans
2 large eggs

MAKES 20

PREPARATION 30 min

COOKING 40 min

DIFFICULTY level 3

Chocolate
wafers

Preheat the oven to 325°F (170°C/gas 3). • Spread the almonds on a large baking sheet. • Toast until pale gold, 5–7 minutes. • Butter four cookie sheets. • Set out two rolling pins. • Sift the flour, cocoa, and salt into a medium bowl. • Use a wooden spoon to mix the egg, egg white, and sugar in a large bowl. • Mix in the dry ingredients and butter. • Drop tablespoons of the mixture 2 inches (5 cm) apart on the prepared cookie sheets. Do not place more than five cookies on each sheet. Spread the mixture out into thin circles. Sprinkle with the almonds. • Bake, one sheet at a time, until firm at the edges, 8–10 minutes. • Working quickly, use a spatula to lift each cookie from the sheet and drape it over a rolling pin. • Let cool completely.

I cup (100 g) flaked almonds
$\frac{1}{3}$ cup (50 g) all-purpose (plain) flour
$\frac{1}{3}$ cup (50 g) unsweetened cocoa powder
$\frac{1}{8}$ teaspoon salt
I large egg + I large egg white
$\frac{1}{2}$ cup (100 g) sugar
$2\frac{1}{2}$ tablespoons butter, softened

Chocolate
honey squares

Preheat the oven to 350°F (180°C/gas 4). • Butter a 10-inch (25-cm) square baking pan. • Melt the chocolate in a double boiler over barely simmering water. • Beat the chocolate, butter, eggs, and honey in a large bowl until well mixed. • Beat in the flour and baking powder. • Spoon the batter into the prepared baking pan. • Bake until well risen and springy to the touch, about 30 minutes. • Let cool in the pan on a rack. • Frosting: beat the confectioners' sugar, cocoa, butter, and water in a large bowl until smooth and glossy. • Spread over the cake and top with walnuts and almonds. • Let the frosting set before cutting into squares.

8 oz (250 g) semisweet (dark) chocolate, chopped
1/3 cup (90 g) butter, softened
4 large eggs
8 oz (250 g) clear honey
1 2/3 cups (250 g) all-purpose (plain) flour
2 teaspoons baking powder
Walnut halves, to decorate
Flaked almonds, to decorate

Frosting
1 2/3 cups (250 g) confectioners' (icing) sugar
1/3 cup (50 g) unsweetened cocoa powder
1/4 cup (60 g) butter, softened
2–3 tablespoons boiling water

MAKES 6–8 servings

PREPARATION 20 min + 12 h to chill

DIFFICULTY level 1

Chocolate
salami slice

Beat the eggs and sugar in a large bowl until pale and creamy. • Beat in the butter and cocoa until well mixed. • Stir in the ladyfingers and the chopped nuts. The dough should be quite firm. • Use your hands to form into a log or salami shape. • Wrap in plastic wrap (cling film) and chill in the refrigerator overnight. • Unwrap and cut into slices about ½-inch (1-cm) thick. • Store in the refrigerator until ready to serve.

1 large egg
1 large egg yolk
⅔ cup (125 g) sugar
½ cup (125 g) butter, melted
½ cup (75 g) unsweetened cocoa powder
30 ladyfingers (or other plain cookies), crumbled
½ cup (50 g) chopped almonds or hazelnuts

MAKES 8–10 servings

PREPARATION 30 min

COOKING 45 min

DIFFICULTY level 2

Chocolate
brownie with vanilla ice cream

Line a 9-inch (23-cm) square baking pan with aluminum foil. Fill with the ice cream in a level layer. Cover and freeze. • Preheat the oven to 350°F (180°C/gas 4). • Butter a 9-inch (23-cm) square baking pan. • Melt the chocolate and butter in a double boiler over barely simmering water. • Add the sugar and mix well. Let cool slightly. • Stir in the eggs, flour, cream, and walnuts. • Spoon the batter into the prepared pan. • Bake until set, about 35 minutes. • Remove from the oven and let cool. • Sauce: Melt the chocolate with the cream, sugar, and coffee in a double boiler over barely simmering water. Remove from the heat and stir in the liqueur. • Drizzle a little of the sauce onto 8–10 individual serving dishes. • Slice the brownie and ice cream into squares about the same size. • Place a slice of brownie on each dish. Cover with a slice of ice cream. Top with another slice of brownie and a slice of ice cream. • Drizzle with a little more of the sauce. Garnish with the raspberries and serve.

1 lb (500 g) vanilla ice cream, softened
1/3 cup (90 g) butter
5 oz (150 g) semisweet (dark) chocolate, chopped
3/4 cup (150 g) firmly packed brown sugar
2 large eggs
1/2 cup (75 g) all-purpose (plain) flour
1/4 cup (60 ml) heavy (double) cream
1/2 cup (50 g) chopped walnuts
Fresh raspberries, to garnish

Sauce
4 oz (125 g) semisweet (dark) chocolate, chopped
1/2 cup (125 ml) heavy (double) cream
1 tablespoon brown sugar
2 tablespoons coffee liqueur
2 teaspoons instant coffee

MAKES about 6–8 servings

PREPARATION 15 min

COOKING 10 min

DIFFICULTY level 1

Chocolate
fondue with fruit

Place the sugar and water into a small saucepan over low heat. Simmer until the sugar has completely dissolved, about 5 minutes. • Melt the chocolate in a double boiler over barely simmering water. Add the butter and stir until smooth and glossy. • Remove from the heat. Stir in the sugar syrup and rum. • Transfer the mixture to a fondue bowl over a flame. • Place this in the center of a large serving dish and arrange the fruit and sponge cake around the edge. Put the chopped nuts into a separate bowl. These can be sprinkled over the fruit after they have been dipped in the chocolate. Vary the fruit according to the season—in summer and fall berry fruit goes very well with chocolate. • Serve hot.

¾ cup (150 g) sugar
½ cup (125 ml water
12 oz (350 g) semisweet (dark) chocolate, broken into pieces
⅓ cup (90 g) butter, softened
1 tablespoon rum

To Serve
1 banana, peeled and cut into bite-size pieces
1 ripe pear, cored, and cut into bite-size pieces
2 mandarins, peeled and broken into segments
2 apricots, peeled, pitted, cut into bite-size pieces
8 strawberries
Dried figs
Candied peel
4 oz (125 g) sponge cake, cut into small cubes
⅓ cup chopped almonds or hazelnuts

MAKES 4 servings

PREPARATION 10 min

DIFFICULTY level 2

Chocolate
vanilla frappé

Melt the chocolate with the water in a double boiler over barely simmering water. • Let cool slightly. Place in a blender with the ice and chop until smooth. • Blend the ice cream and milk separately. • Pour the two mixtures gradually into chilled glasses, pouring them both at the same time to create a marbled pattern in each glass. • Garnish with chocolate flakes and wafers. • Serve immediately.

8 oz (250 g) semisweet (dark) chocolate, broken into pieces + extra, flaked, to garnish

Generous ¾ cup (200 ml) hot water

8 ice cubes

8 oz (250 g) vanilla ice cream

⅔ cup (150 ml) milk

8 "cigarette" shaped wafers, to garnish

MAKES 4–6 servings

PREPARATION 10 min

COOKING 10 min

DIFFICULTY level 1

Chocolate Sundae
with strawberries and cream

Beat the cornstarch and milk in a medium saucepan. • Add about $\frac{1}{2}$ cup (125 ml) of the cream and all the chocolate. Simmer over low heat, stirring constantly, until the chocolate is melted and the mixture is slightly thickened, about 10 minutes. Remove from the heat and let cool. • Whip the remaining cream in a large bowl until stiff. • Layer the cream, chocolate mixture, and strawberries in sundae dishes and serve.

2 tablespoons cornstarch (cornflour)

Scant $1\frac{1}{4}$ cups (300 ml) milk

$1\frac{2}{3}$ cups (400 ml) double (heavy) cream

8 oz (250 g) semisweet (dark) chocolate, broken into pieces

14 oz (400 g) fresh strawberries, sliced

MAKES 6 servings

PREPARATION 35 min + 2 h to set

COOKING 10 min

DIFFICULTY level 2

Chocolate Slab

with cream and raspberries

Melt the chocolate in a double boiler over barely simmering water.
• Pour the melted chocolate over a large sheet of waxed paper and
spread to a thickness of $\frac{1}{8}$ inch (3 mm). • Let stand until set. • Cut
the sheet into 18 rectangles of equal size using a sharp knife dipped
in boiling water. • Beat the cream and sugar in a large bowl until stiff.
• Refrigerate until ready to use. • Place a rectangle of chocolate on
each serving dish. Top with a spoonful of cream and a few
raspberries. Cover with another piece of chocolate, more cream
and raspberries and finish with another layer of chocolate. •
Decorate with the mint leaves and raspberries. Dust with the
confectioners' sugar.

14 oz (400 g) semisweet (dark) chocolate

$1\frac{1}{4}$ cups (310 ml) heavy (double) cream

4 tablespoons sugar

14 oz (400 g) fresh raspberries

1 tablespoon coarsely chopped mint, to garnish

$\frac{1}{3}$ cup (50 g) confectioners' (icing) sugar, to dust

Chocolate
vanilla custard

Preheat the oven to 350°F (180°C/gas 4). • Butter a 9 x 5-inch (23 x 12-cm) loaf pan. Wrap the outside in aluminum foil, to make it waterproof. • Melt the butter in a large saucepan over low heat. Add the flour and milk. Simmer, stirring constantly, until thickened, about 5 minutes. Let cool. • Beat the eggs, egg yolks, and sugar in a small bowl until pale and creamy. • Stir into the milk mixture. • Divide the mixture between 2 bowls. • Stir the vanilla into one bowl and the cocoa into the other. • Pour half the chocolate mixture into the pan. Top the vanilla mixture and then the remaining chocolate mixture. • Place the pan in a larger pan of cold water and bake until set, 1 hour. Let cool completely. • Sauce: Bring the milk and coconut to a boil in a saucepan over low heat. Let cool. • Filter through a fine mesh strainer. • Beat the egg yolks, sugar, cinnamon, and flour in a bowl. Gradually beat in the milk. Return to the saucepan and bring to a boil, stirring constantly, until thickened. Let cool. • Turn the custard out onto a serving dish. Serve with the sauce.

1/3 cup (90 g) butter
2/3 cup (100 g) all-purpose (plain) flour
2 cups (500 ml) milk
4 large eggs
2 large egg yolks
1/2 cup (100 g) sugar
1 teaspoon vanilla extract (essence)
1/4 cup (30 g) unsweetened cocoa powder

Sauce
1 2/3 cups (400 ml) milk
3/4 cup (90 g) desiccated coconut
2 large egg yolks
2 tablespoons sugar
1/2 teaspoon ground cinnamon
1 tablespoon all-purpose (plain) flour

MAKES 6–8 servings

PREPARATION 30 min

COOKING 10 min

DIFFICULTY level 1

Strawberries
dipped in chocolate

Bring the cream to a boil in a large saucepan over low heat. Remove from the heat. • Add the butter and chocolate. Stir until the chocolate has melted and the mixture is smooth and glossy. • Dip the strawberries into the chocolate so that they are half-coated. • Place on a sheet of waxed paper and let the chocolate set. • Dip in the chocolate again. • Place the strawberries in mini cupcake cases and let the chocolate set.

Generous ¾ cup (200 ml) heavy (double) cream
Generous ⅓ cup (100 g) butter
8 oz (250 g) semisweet (dark) chocolate, broken into pieces
1 lb (500 g) ripe strawberries

Chocolate
bavarian cream

Bring the milk to a boil in a small saucepan over low heat. • Beat the sugar and egg yolks in a medium bowl until pale and creamy. • Slowly pour the milk into the egg mixture, beating constantly. • Return to the saucepan and bring to a boil. Remove from the heat just before it boils. • Let cool for 5 minutes then add the chocolate and gelatin and stir until dissolved. • Let cool. • Place the sponge cake in 9-inch (23-cm) springform pan. • Brush with the rum. • Beat the cream until stiff and fold it into the chocolate mixture. • Spoon the mixture into the pan over the sponge. Chill in the refrigerator until set, about 4 hours. • Decorate with the grated chocolate just before serving.

⅔ cup (180 ml) milk
½ cup (100 g) sugar
4 large egg yolks
4 oz (125 g) semisweet (dark) chocolate
1 tablespoon gelatin powder
1 (9-inch/23-cm) storebought sponge cake, about 1-inch (2.5-cm) high
2 tablespoons rum
2 cups (500 ml) heavy (double) cream
Grated semisweet (dark) and white chocolate, to garnish

Mocha Mousse

Preheat the oven to 350°F (180°C/gas 4). • Oil a 4-cup (1-liter) pudding mold. • Heat the milk in a medium saucepan over low heat. Add the coffee and stir until dissolved. Remove from the heat and stir in the liqueur. • Beat the sugar, eggs, and egg yolks in a large bowl until pale and creamy. • Beat in the cocoa and, gradually, the milk mixture. • Pour the mixture into the prepared pudding mold. • Place the mold in a larger pan of cold water and bake in the oven until set, about 1 hour. • Let cool at room temperature then chill in the refrigerator for at least 4 hours. • Beat the cream with the confectioners' sugar until stiff. • Decorate the mousse with the cream, grated chocolate, and coffee beans just before serving.

2 cups (500 ml) milk

2 tablespoons instant coffee

1/4 cup (60 ml) coffee liqueur

3/4 cup (150 g) sugar

4 large eggs

4 large egg yolks

4 tablespoons unsweetened cocoa powder

1/2 cup (125 ml) heavy (double) cream

1 tablespoon confectioners' (icing) sugar

2 oz (60 g) semisweet (dark) chocolate, grated

Coffee beans

MAKES 8–10 servings

PREPARATION 30 min + 6 h to chill

COOKING 15 min

DIFFICULTY level 2

Ladyfinger
mousse

Butter a 10-inch (25-cm) springform pan. • Melt the chocolate in a double boiler over barely simmering water. Let cool. • Dissolve the sugar in $\frac{1}{2}$ cup (125 ml) water in a saucepan over medium heat. Wash down the pan sides with a pastry brush dipped in cold water to prevent sugar crystals from forming. Cook, without stirring, until the mixture reaches 238°F (114°C), or the soft-ball stage. • Beat the eggs and egg yolks in a large bowl with an electric mixer at medium speed until frothy. With mixer at high speed, gradually add the sugar mixture, beating until thick. • Sprinkle the gelatin over the remaining water in a small saucepan. Let stand 1 minute. Simmer over low heat until completely dissolved. • Add the gelatin mixture to the egg mixture. • With mixer at high speed, beat the cream in a large bowl until stiff. • Use a large rubber spatula to fold in the chocolate and then the cream. • Cover the pan with a layer of ladyfingers. • Spoon the mousse over the top and refrigerate for 6 hours, or until set. Carefully remove the pan sides just before serving.

1 lb (500 g) bittersweet (dark) chocolate
$1\frac{1}{4}$ cups (250 g) sugar
1 cup (200 ml) water
2 large eggs
8 large egg yolks
1 tablespoon unflavored gelatin
$1\frac{1}{2}$ cups (375 ml) heavy (double) cream
36 ladyfingers

MAKES 6–8 servings

PREPARATION 30 min

COOKING 1 h

DIFFICULTY level 1

Meringue Cake
with chocolate filling

Meringues: Preheat the oven to 250°F (130°C/gas $1/2$). • Line a baking sheet with parchment paper and mark two 9-inch (23-cm) circles on the paper. • Beat the egg whites in a large bowl with an electric mixer at medium speed until frothy. • With mixer at high speed, gradually beat in the confectioners' sugar until stiff, glossy peaks form. • Spoon the mixture into a pastry bag with a plain $1/2$-inch (1-cm) nozzle and pipe into two spiral disks, starting at the center and filling each 9-inch (23-cm) circle. • Bake until crisp and dry, about 1 hour. Turn off the oven and leave the door ajar until the meringues are completely cool. • Chocolate Pastry Cream: Beat the egg yolks and sugar with an electric mixer at high speed until pale and thick. • Bring the milk to a boil with the salt and vanilla, then stir it into the egg and sugar. • Simmer over low heat, stirring constantly with a wooden spoon until thick, about 10 minutes. Stir in the chocolate. • Topping: With mixer at high speed, beat the cream, sugar, and vanilla in a small bowl until stiff. • To Assemble: Carefully remove the parchment paper from the meringues. Place one layer on a serving plate. Spread with the pastry cream. Top with the remaining meringue layer. • Spread with the cream topping and decorate with the meringues and strawberries.

Meringues
5 large egg whites,
    at room temperature
$1^1/2$ cups (225 g) confectioners' (icing)
    sugar

Chocolate Pastry Cream
5 large egg yolks
$3/4$ cup (150 g) sugar
$1/3$ cup (50 g) all-purpose (plain) flour
2 cups (500 ml) milk
$1/4$ teaspoon salt
1 teaspoon vanilla extract (essence)
8 oz (250 g) semisweet (dark) chocolate

Topping
1 cup (250 ml) heavy (double) cream
1 tablespoon sugar
$1/2$ teaspoon vanilla extract (essence)
8 mini meringues
    (storebought or homemade)
Fresh strawberries, to decorate

Black Forest Cake

Chocolate Cake: Preheat the oven to 350°F (180°C/gas 4). • Butter two 9-inch (23-cm) round cake pans. Line with waxed paper. Butter the paper. • Sift the flour, baking powder, and salt into a large bowl. • Melt the chocolate and water in a double boiler over barely simmering water. Set aside to cool. • Beat the butter and brown sugar in a large bowl with an electric mixer at medium speed until creamy. • Add the eggs, one at a time, beating until just blended after each addition. • With mixer at low speed, gradually beat in the chocolate mixture, sour cream, and dry ingredients. • Spoon half the batter into each of the prepared pans. • Bake until a toothpick inserted into the centers comes out clean, about 45 minutes. • Cool the cakes in the pans for 10 minutes. Turn out onto racks. Carefully remove the waxed paper and let cool completely. • Split the cakes in half horizontally. • Filling: Mix the cherry preserves and kirsch. • With mixer at high speed, beat the cream in a medium bowl until stiff. • Frosting: Melt the chocolate and butter in a double boiler over barely simmering water. • To Assemble: Place a layer of cake on a serving plate. Spread with one-third of the cherry preserves mixture and one-third of the whipped cream. Repeat with the remaining cake layers, finishing with a plain layer. Spread the frosting over the top and sides of the cake. Decorate with the candied cherries.

Chocolate Cake
1⅔ cups (250 g) all-purpose (plain) flour
1½ teaspoons baking powder
¼ teaspoon salt
5 oz (150 g) semisweet (dark) chocolate, coarsely chopped
½ cup (125 ml) water
½ cup (125 g) butter
1¼ cups (250 g) firmly packed brown sugar
2 large eggs
½ cup (125 ml) sour cream

Filling
1½ cups (480 ml) cherry preserves (jam)
3 tablespoons kirsch (cherry schnapps)
2 cups (500 ml) heavy (double) cream

Frosting
8 oz (250 g) bittersweet (dark) chocolate, coarsely chopped
4 tablespoons butter
Candied cherries, to decorate

MAKES 8–10 servings

PREPARATION 20 min + 1 h to cool

COOKING 1 h

DIFFICULTY level 2

White Chocolate

ring with creamy frosting

Preheat the oven to 325°F (175°C/gas 3). • Oil a 9-inch (23-cm) ring pan. • Place the milk, sugar, chocolate, and butter in a saucepan over low heat. Stir constantly until the mixture is smooth and creamy. Do not let it boil. Remove from the heat. Let cool. • Beat in the flour, baking powder, vanilla, and eggs until smooth. • Spoon the batter into the prepared pan. • Bake until a toothpick inserted into the center comes out clean, about 1 hour. • Let cool in the pan for 15 minutes. Turn out onto the rack and let cool completely. • Frosting: Bring the cream to a boil in a saucepan over low heat. Remove from the heat and add the chocolate. Stir until the chocolate has melted. • Chill in the refrigerator for 30 minutes. • Place the cake on a serving dish. Drizzle with the frosting. Garnish with pieces of candied orange. • Chill until ready to serve.

1 cup (250 ml) milk
2¼ cups (450 g) sugar
5 oz (150 g) white chocolate, chopped
1 cup (250 g) butter
2 cups (300 g) all-purpose (plain) flour
2 teaspoons baking powder
1 teaspoon extract (essence)
2 large eggs, lightly beaten
Candied orange, to garnish

Frosting
½ cup (125 ml) heavy (double) cream
12 oz (350 g) white chocolate, chopped

MAKES 8–10 servings

PREPARATION 15 min

COOKING 45 min

DIFFICULTY level 2

Chocolate Cake

with creamy frosting

Preheat the oven to 350°F (180°C/gas 4). • Butter and flour a 9-inch (23-cm) springform pan. • Sift the flour, cocoa, and baking powder into a large bowl. • Beat the butter and sugar with an electric mixer at medium speed until creamy. • Add the egg yolks, one at a time, until just blended after each addition. • With mixer at low speed, gradually beat in the dry ingredients. • Beat the egg whites and salt until stiff peaks form. Use a large rubber spatula to fold them into the batter. • Spoon the batter into the prepared pan. • Bake until a toothpick inserted into the center comes out clean, about 45 minutes. • Cool the cake in the pan for 5 minutes. Loosen and remove the pan sides. Invert onto a rack and remove the pan bottom. Let cool completely. • Dust with the cocoa powder. • Frosting: Melt the chocolate, butter, and condensed milk in a double boiler over barely simmering water. • Spread the top and sides of the cake with frosting, finishing with a lattice pattern, if liked. Stick the sides of the cake with the grated chocolate.

1²⁄₃ cups (250 g) all-purpose (plain) flour

¹⁄₃ cup (50 g) unsweetened cocoa powder

1 teaspoon baking powder

³⁄₄ cup (180 g) butter, softened

³⁄₄ cup (150 g) sugar

2 large eggs, separated

¹⁄₈ teaspoon salt

Frosting

6 oz (180 g) semisweet (dark) chocolate, coarsely chopped

¹⁄₃ cup (90 g) butter

¹⁄₂ cup (125 ml) sweetened condensed milk

6 oz (180 g) semisweet (dark) chocolate, coarsely grated, to decorate

MAKES 8–10 servings

PREPARATION 20 min

COOKING 50 min

DIFFICULTY level 1

Chocolate Ring
with chocolate sauce

Preheat the oven to 350°F (180°C/gas 4). • Butter and flour a 9-inch (23-cm) ring pan. • Sift the flour, cocoa, baking powder, baking soda, and salt into a large bowl. Stir in the sugars. • Beat the butter, milk, eggs, coffee mixture, and vanilla in a large bowl with an electric mixer at medium speed until well blended. With mixer at low speed, beat the butter mixture into the dry ingredients. • Spoon the batter into the pan. • Bake until a toothpick inserted into the center comes out clean, about 50 minutes. • Cool the cake in the pan for 15 minutes. Turn out onto a rack to cool completely. • Chocolate Sauce: Stir the chocolate and cream in a small saucepan over very low heat until the chocolate melts. Remove from the heat. Set aside to cool. • Spoon the sauce over the cake and serve with raspberries.

1⅓ cups (200 g) all-purpose (plain) flour
⅓ cup (50 g) unsweetened cocoa powder
1 teaspoon baking powder
1 teaspoon baking soda
¼ teaspoon salt
¾ cup (150 g) sugar
⅓ cup (70 g) firmly packed dark brown sugar
¼ cup (60 g) butter, melted
1 cup (250 ml) milk
2 large eggs, at room temperature
1 tablespoon instant coffee, dissolved in 1 tablespoon milk
1 teaspoon vanilla extract (essence)

Chocolate Sauce
4 oz (125 g) bittersweet chocolate chips
½ cup (125 ml) heavy (double) cream
Raspberries, to serve

Devil's Food
cake

Preheat the oven to 350°F (180°C/gas 4). • Butter two 9-inch (23-cm) round cake pans. Line with waxed paper. Butter the paper. • Melt the chocolate in a double boiler over barely simmering water. Set aside to cool. • Stir together the milk and lemon juice to make sour milk. Set aside. • Sift the flour, baking powder, baking soda, and salt into a large bowl. • Beat both sugars, butter, and vanilla in a large bowl with an electric mixer at medium speed until creamy. • Add the eggs, one at a time, beating until just blended after each addition. • With mixer at low speed, gradually beat in the dry ingredients, food coloring, and chocolate, alternating with the sour milk. • Spoon the batter into the prepared pans. • Bake until a toothpick inserted into the centers comes out clean, about 35 minutes. • Cool the cakes in the pans for 5 minutes. Turn out onto racks. Carefully remove the waxed paper and let cool completely. • Mock cream: Beat the butter, sugar, water, and vanilla in a large bowl with an electric mixer at high speed until thick and creamy. The mixture may curdle as you beat; continue beating until smooth. • Rich Chocolate Frosting: Bring the sugar and 1 cup (250 ml) cream to a boil in a saucepan over medium heat. Simmer for 1 minute, then remove from the heat. • Stir in the chocolate. • Return the saucepan to medium heat and cook, without stirring, until the mixture reaches 238°F (114°C), or the soft-ball stage. Remove from the heat. • Add the butter and vanilla, without stirring, and place the saucepan in a larger pan of cold water for 5 minutes before stirring. • Beat until the frosting begins to lose its sheen, 5–10 minutes. Stir in 1 tablespoon of cream. Stir until smooth and spreadable. • Place one cake on a serving plate. Spread with the raspberry preserves, followed by the Mock Cream. Top with the remaining cake. • Spread the top and sides with frosting.

Cake
5 oz (150 g) semisweet (dark) chocolate
1 cup (250 ml) milk
1 tablespoon lemon juice
2 cups (300 g) all-purpose (plain) flour
1 teaspoon baking powder
1/2 teaspoon baking soda
1/4 teaspoon salt
3/4 cup (150 g) sugar
3/4 cup (150 g) firmly packed brown sugar
1/2 cup (125 g) butter
1 teaspoon vanilla extract (essence)
2 large eggs
1 teaspoon red food coloring
1/2 cup (160 ml) raspberry preserves (jam)

Mock Cream
1/2 cup (125 g) butter, softened
1/2 cup (100 g) sugar
1/2 cup (125 ml) boiling water
1 teaspoon vanilla extract (essence)

Rich Chocolate Frosting
2 cups (400 g) sugar
1 cup (250 ml) heavy (double) cream + 1–2 tablespoons as needed
8 oz (250 g) bittersweet (dark) chocolate, coarsely chopped
2 tablespoons butter
1 teaspoon vanilla extract (essence)

MAKES 8–10 servings

PREPARATION 25 min

COOKING 1 h

DIFFICULTY level 2

White Chocolate
mud cake

Preheat the oven to 325°F (170°C/gas 3). • Butter and flour a 9-inch (23-cm) springform pan. • Stir the butter, chocolate, brown sugar, milk, and corn syrup in a large saucepan over low heat until smooth. Do not boil. Set aside to cool. • Stir in the flour and baking powder. Add the eggs, one at a time, beating until just blended after each addition. • Spoon the batter into the prepared pan. • Bake for about until a toothpick inserted into the center comes out clean, about 50 minutes. • Cool the cake in the pan for 10 minutes. Loosen and remove the pan sides. Invert the cake onto a rack. Loosen and remove the pan bottom and let cool completely. • White Chocolate Ganache: Heat the cream almost to a boil in a small saucepan over low heat. • Place the chocolate in a large bowl. Pour the cream over the chocolate and stir until the chocolate is melted and smooth. • Refrigerate until thick and spreadable, about 30 minutes, stirring occasionally. • Spread the top and sides of the cake with the ganache.

Mud Cake
- ¾ cup (180 g) butter
- 5 oz (150 g) white chocolate, coarsely chopped
- 1 cup (200 g) firmly packed light brown sugar
- 1 cup (250 ml) milk
- 6 tablespoons corn (golden) syrup
- 2 cups (300 g) all-purpose (plain) flour
- 2 teaspoons baking powder
- 2 large eggs

White Chocolate Ganache
- ½ cup (125 ml) heavy (double) cream
- 12 oz (350 g) white chocolate, coarsely chopped

MAKES 8–10 servings

PREPARATION 20 min + 6 h to chill

COOKING 1 h

DIFFICULTY level 2

Chocolate Chip

cheesecake with amaretto

Preheat the oven to 400°F (200°C/gas 6). • Butter a 10-inch (25-cm) springform pan. • Mix the crumbs, almonds, and butter in a medium bowl. • Press into the bottom and partway up the sides of the prepared pan. • Bake until lightly browned, 8–10 minutes. Cool the crust in the pan on a rack. • Filling: Beat the cream cheese, sugar, and cornstarch in a large bowl with an electric mixer at medium speed until smooth. • Add the eggs, one at a time, beating until just blended after each addition. • With mixer at low speed, beat in the amaretto and vanilla. Stir in the chocolate chips. • Spoon the filling into the crust. • Bake until set, about 1 hour. • Cool the cake in the pan on a rack. Chill in the refrigerator for at least 6 hours. • Loosen and remove the pan sides to serve.

Cheesecake
2 cups (150 g) crushed amaretti cookies
1/2 cup (75 g) almonds, finely chopped
1/2 cup (125 g) butter, melted

Filling
8 oz (250 g) cream cheese, softened
1 cup (200 g) sugar
2 tablespoons cornstarch (cornflour)
3 large eggs, at room temperature
3 tablespoons amaretto liqueur
1 teaspoon vanilla extract (essence)
1 cup (200 g) semisweet (dark) chocolate chips

Chocolate Pie

Preheat the oven to 400°F (200°C/gas 6). • Butter and flour a 10-inch (25-cm) springform pan. • Bring the cream to a boil in a large saucepan over low heat. Remove from the heat, add the chocolate, and stir until completely melted. Let cool. • Stir in the milk and eggs. • Roll out the pastry on a lightly floured work surface. Line the prepared pan. Prick the base with a fork. • Line the pastry case with waxed paper. Fill it with dry beans or pie weights and bake blind for 10 minutes. • Remove the beans and waxed paper. • Fill the case with the chocolate filling and bake until the filling has set, 20–25 minutes. • Let cool. • Loosen and remove the sides of the pan. • Decorate with the whipped cream and raspberries.

10 oz (300 g) frozen shortcrust pastry, thawed

2 cups (500 ml) heavy (double) cream

1 lb (500 g) semisweet (dark) chocolate, broken into pieces

Generous ³⁄₄ cup (200 ml) milk

3 large eggs, lightly beaten

¹⁄₂ cup (125 ml) whipped cream, to decorate

Fresh raspberries, to decorate

MAKES 6–8 servings

PREPARATION 30 min

COOKING 25 min

DIFFICULTY level 2

Chocolate
roulade

Preheat the oven to 350°F (180°C/gas 4). • Butter a 14 x 10-inch (35 x 25-cm) jelly roll pan. Line with parchment paper. • Melt the chocolate in a double boiler over barely simmering water. • Remove from the heat. • Beat the egg yolks and sugar in a large bowl until pale and creamy. • Add the melted chocolate and mix well. • Beat the egg whites and salt in a large bowl until stiff. • Fold into the chocolate egg yolk mixture. • Spoon the batter into the prepared pan. • Bake until springy to the touch, 15–20 minutes. Let cool in the pan on a rack for 5 minutes. • Turn out onto a clean kitchen towel. • Discard the baking parchment. Trim off the crisp edges of the cake. • Roll up the cake using the towel as a guide. Let cool. • Filling: Whip the cream and sugar in a large bowl until stiff. • Stir in the cocoa and liqueur. • Unroll the cooled cake and spread with half the filling. Roll up and place on a serving dish. • Spread with the remaining filling.

8 oz (250 g) semisweet (dark) chocolate, chopped
8 large eggs, separated
1 1/4 cups (250 g) sugar
1/4 teaspoon salt

Filling
1 1/2 cups (375 ml) heavy (double) cream
2 tablespoons sugar
4 tablespoons unsweetened cocoa powder
2 tablespoons orange liqueur

MAKES 6–8 servings

PREPARATION 30 min + 4 h to chill

COOKING 15 min

DIFFICULTY level 1

Chocolate Pie
with berries

Mix the crumbs, almonds, and butter in a large bowl. • Press into the bottom and partway up the sides of a 9-inch (23-cm) pie plate. • Chill in the refrigerator until set, about 2 hours. • Spoon the pastry cream into the pastry and chill in the refrigerator for 2 hours. • Decorate with the fruit. • Heat the apricot preserves in a small pan until liquid. Brush the pie with the preserves.

- 1½ cups (200 g) finely crushed Graham's crackers or digestive biscuits
- ⅔ cup (90 g) almonds, finely ground
- ¾ cup (180 g) butter, melted
- 1 quantity Chocolate pastry cream (see page 42)
- 12 oz (350 g) cups mixed berries
- ¼ cup (60 g) apricot preserves (jam)

MAKES 8–10 servings

PREPARATION 45 min

COOKING 20 min

DIFFICULTY level 2

White Chocolate
thousand-layer cake

Preheat the oven to 400°F (200°C/gas 6). • Cut out five 9-inch (23-cm) disks of waxed paper. • Roll out the pastry very thinly on a lightly floured work surface. Cut into five 9-inch (23-cm) disks. Place on the waxed paper and prick all over with a fork. • Bake until pale golden brown, 15–20 minutes. • Sprinkle each piece of pastry with 1 tablespoon of confectioners' sugar and return to the oven to caramelize, about 5 minutes. • Cool the pastry on racks. • Place one pastry layer on a serving plate and spread with pastry cream. Repeat until the pastry cream and pastry is all used up, reserving a little pastry cream to decorate. • Melt the bittersweet chocolate in a double boiler over barely simmering water. Set aside to cool. • Spread the top of the cake with the melted chocolate. Decorate with the remaining pastry cream.

1½ lb (750 g) frozen puff pastry, thawed

5 tablespoons confectioners' (icing) sugar

1½ quantities Chocolate Pastry Cream (see page 42), made with white chocolate instead of semisweet (dark) chocolate

4 oz (125 g) bittersweet (dark) chocolate, coarsely chopped

MAKES 6–8 servings

PREPARATION 20 min

COOKING 55 min

DIFFICULTY level 2

Chocolate Loaf

with cream and strawberries

Preheat the oven to 400°F (200°C/gas 6). • Butter a 9 x 5-inch (23 x 12-cm) loaf pan. • Melt 4 oz (125 g) of the chocolate in a double boiler over barely simmering water. • Beat the 3 whole eggs with half the sugar in a large bowl until pale and creamy. Stir in the chocolate. • Fold in the almonds and half the flour. • Spoon the batter into the pan. Bake until springy to the touch, 45 minutes. Let cool slightly then turn out onto a rack to cool completely. • Beat the egg yolks and remaining sugar in a large bowl until pale and creamy. Stir in the remaining flour. • Bring the milk to a boil over low heat. Add the milk to the egg mixture. Beat well and return to the saucepan. • Simmer over low heat, stirring constantly, until thickened, about 5 minutes. Remove from the heat and stir in the remaining chocolate. Let cool. • Slice the cake horizontally into 3 layers. • Place a layer on a serving dish. Spread with half the custard. Cover with strawberries. Cover with another layer of cake and remaining custard. Top with the remaining strawberries. Cover with the last layer of cake. Dust with cocoa and garnish with strawberries.

5 oz (150 g) semisweet (dark) chocolate, chopped
3 large eggs
1 cup (200 g) sugar
1 cup (100 g) ground almonds
2/3 cup (100 g) all-purpose (plain) flour
4 egg yolks, lightly beaten
1 2/3 cups (400 ml) milk
12 oz (350 g) strawberries, sliced
1 tablespoon unsweetened cocoa powder
Strawberries, dipped in caramelized sugar, to garnish (optional)

MAKES 6–8 servings

PREPARATION 20 min

COOKING 45 min

DIFFICULTY level 1

Vienna Cake

Preheat the oven to 350°F (180°C/gas 4). • Butter a 9 x 5-inch (23 x 12-cm) loaf pan. • Melt the butter in a large saucepan with the sugar and chocolate over low heat. Stir until smooth and glossy. • Add the almonds and mix well. Let cool, stirring from time to time. • Beat in the egg yolks one at a time. • Stir in the flour and baking powder. • Beat the egg whites in a large bowl until stiff. Fold into the chocolate mixture. • Spoon the batter into the prepared pan. • Bake until springy to the touch, about 45 minutes. • Let cool slightly then turn out onto a rack to cool completely. • Frosting: Beat the confectioners' sugar, lemon juice, orange juice, and rum in a bowl. • Drizzle the frosting over the cake. Decorate with the candied orange.

1/2 cup (125 g) butter
3/4 cup (150 g) sugar
5 oz (150 g) dark chocolate, broken into pieces
3/4 cup (75 g) ground almonds
4 large eggs, separated
Generous 1/3 cup (60 g) all-purpose (plain) flour
1 teaspoon baking powder
2 tablespoons chopped candied peel, to decorate

Frosting
1 1/3 cups (200 g) confectioners' (icing) sugar
1 teaspoon lemon juice
2 tablespoons orange juice
1 tablespoon rum

Index

Copyright © 2007 by McRae Books Srl

This English edition first published in 2007

Chocolate

was created and produced by McRae Books Srl

Borgo Santa Croce, 8 – Florence (Italy)

info@mcraebooks.com

Publishers: Anne McRae and Marco Nardi

Project Director: Anne McRae

Design: Sara Mathews

Text: Carla Bardi

Editing: Osla Fraser

Photography: Cristina Canepari, Keeho Casati, Gil Gallo, Walter Mericchi, Sandra Preussinger

Home Economist: Benedetto Rillo

Artbuying: McRae Books

Layouts: Adina Stefania Dragomir

Repro: Fotolito Raf, Florence

ISBN 978-88-89272-87-9

Printed and bound in China